ANIMALS
That Make a Difference!

Tigers

Ashley Lee

Explore other books at:
WWW.ENGAGEBOOKS.COM

VANCOUVER, B.C.

℮ ↗ WWW.ENGAGEBOOKS.COM

Tigers: Pre-1
Animals That Make a Difference!
Lee, Ashley, 1995
Text © 2025 Engage Books
Design © 2025 Engage Books

Edited by: A.R. Roumanis, and Ashley Lee
Design by: Mandy Christiansen

Text set in Arial Regular.

FIRST EDITION / FIRST PRINTING

library and archives canada cataloguing in publication

Title: Tigers / Ashley Lee.
Names: Lee, Ashley, author.
Description: Series statement: Animals that make a difference

Identifiers: Canadiana (print) 20230448542 | Canadiana (ebook) 20230448569
ISBN 978-1-77878-693-8 (hardcover)
ISBN 978-1-77878-702-7 (softcover)

Subjects:
LCSH: Tigers—Juvenile literature.
LCSH: Human-animal relationships—Juvenile literature.

Classification: LCC QL737.P94 C38 2025 | DDC J599.885—DC23

This project has been made possible in part by the Government of Canada.

Canada

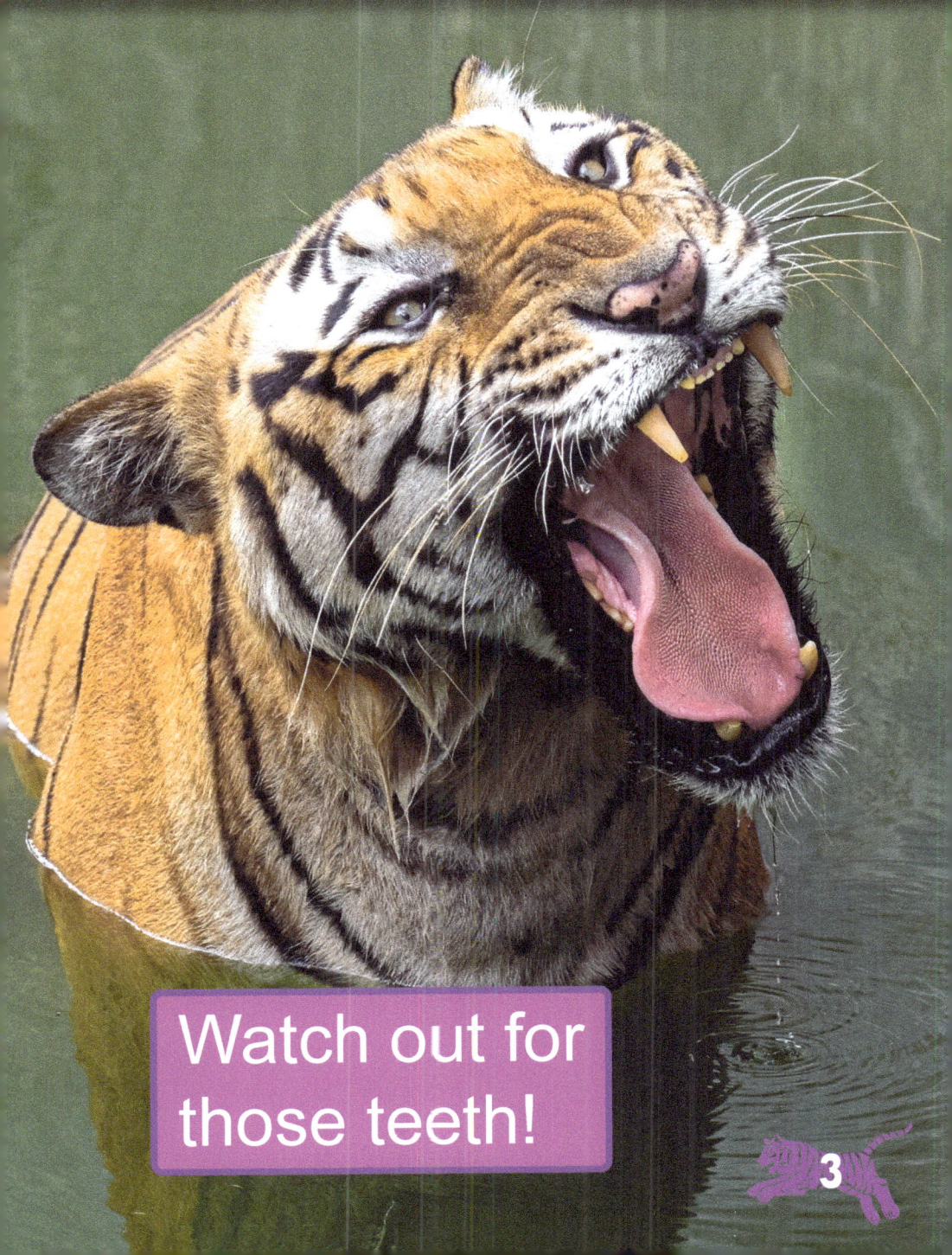

Watch out for those teeth!

Tigers are a kind
of big cat.

4

They are the biggest
cats in the world.

Most tigers are orange and white with dark stripes.

Tigers have
sharp claws.

They also have large teeth.

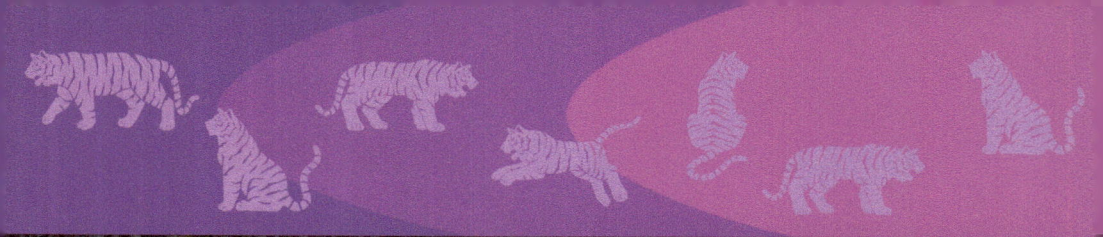

Tigers live in Asia and Russia.

Most like to live alone.

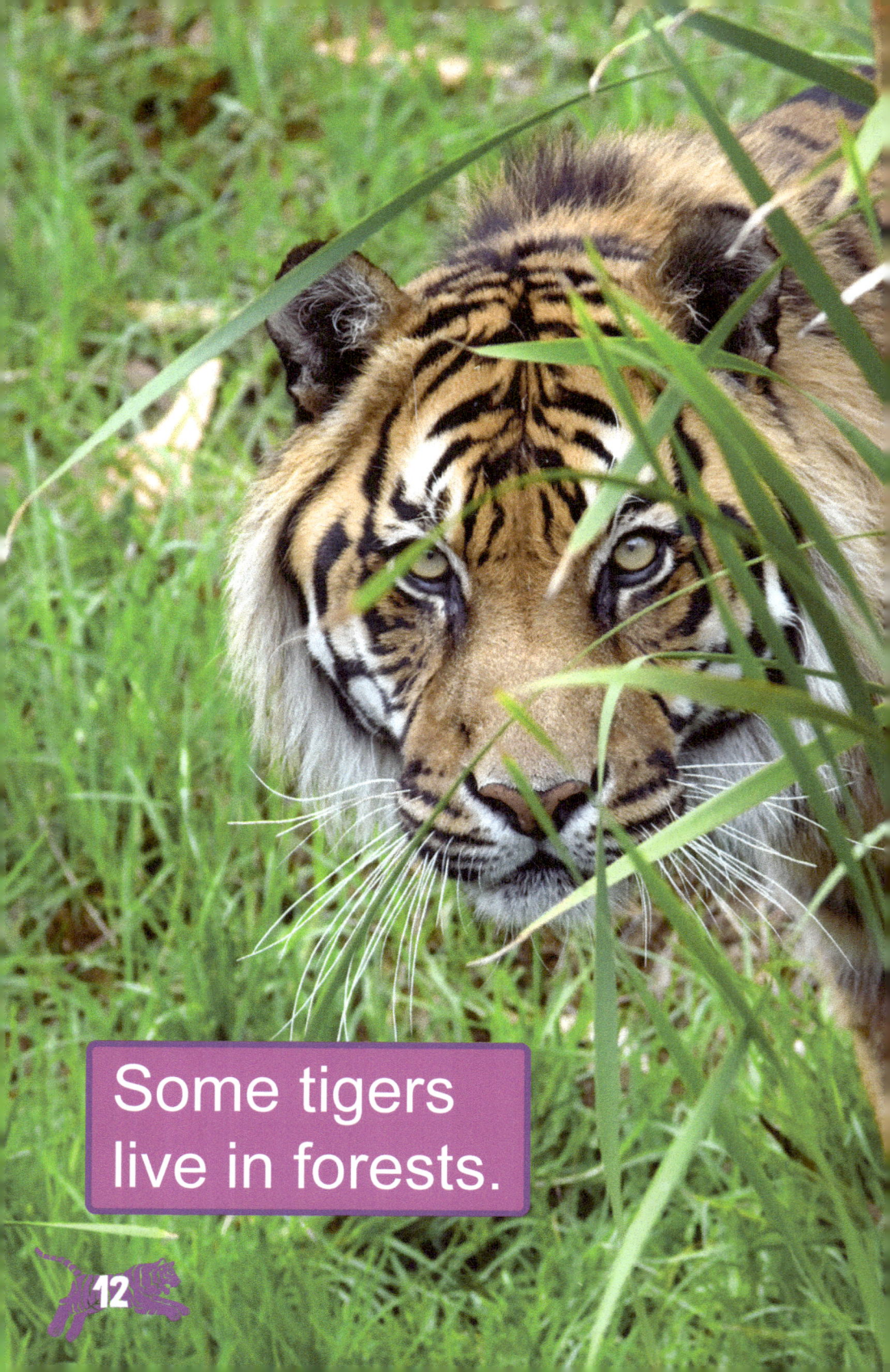

Some tigers
live in forests.

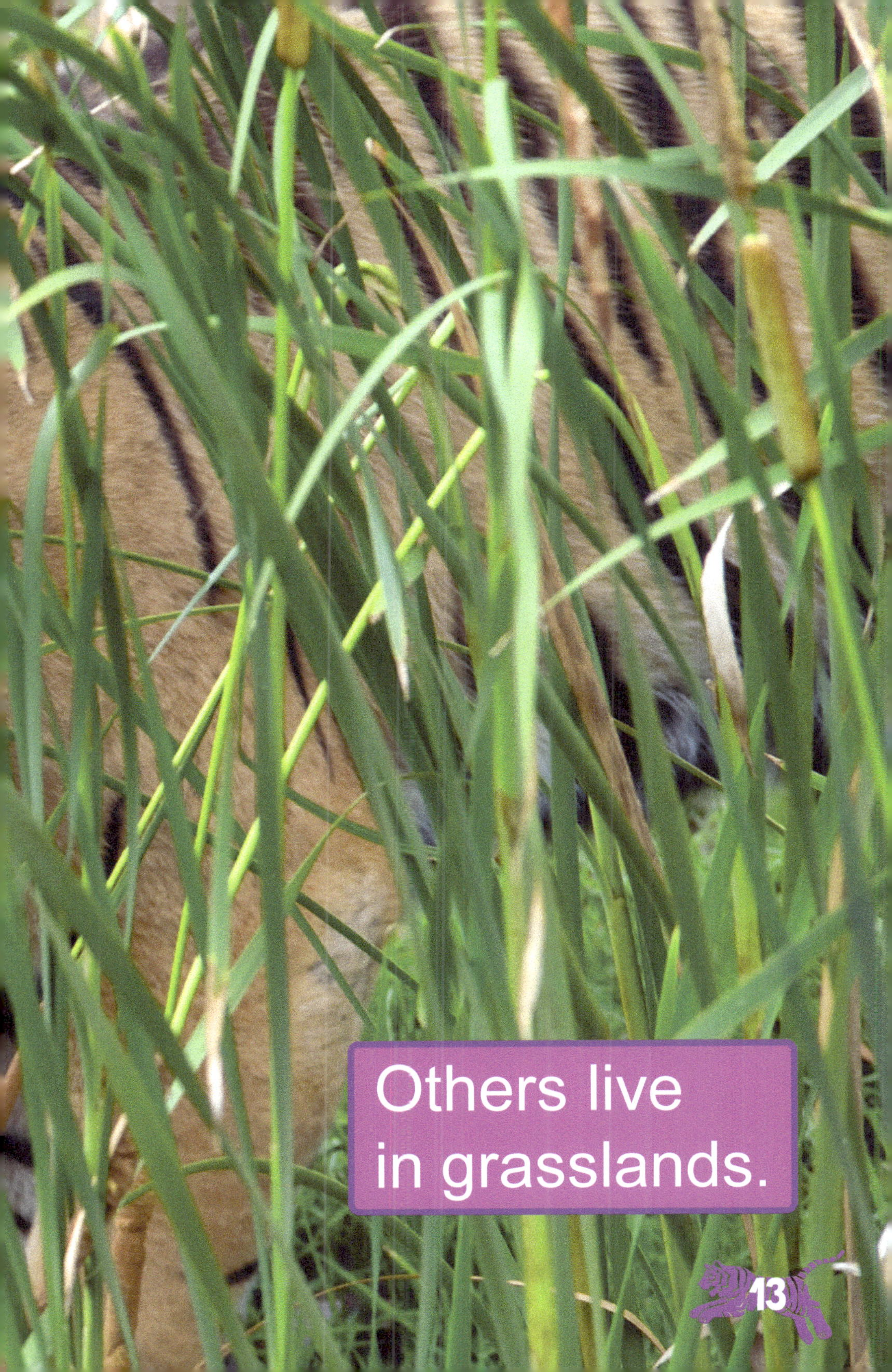

Others live
in grasslands.

Tigers leave smells around their homes to tell others to stay away.

15

Tigers eat other animals.

They often eat deer or pigs.

17

Too many deer and pigs will eat all the plants.

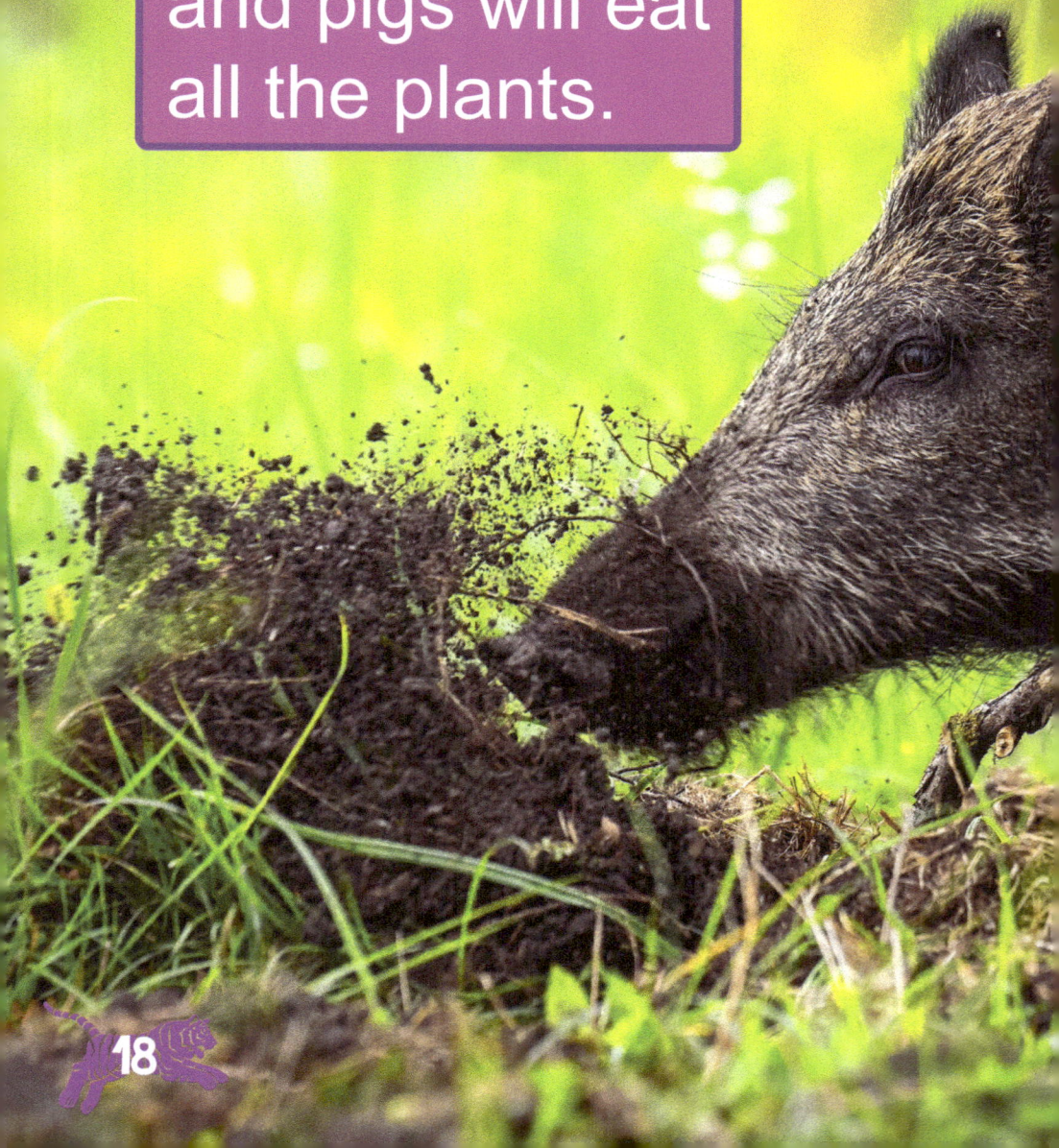

Eating these animals keeps their numbers down.

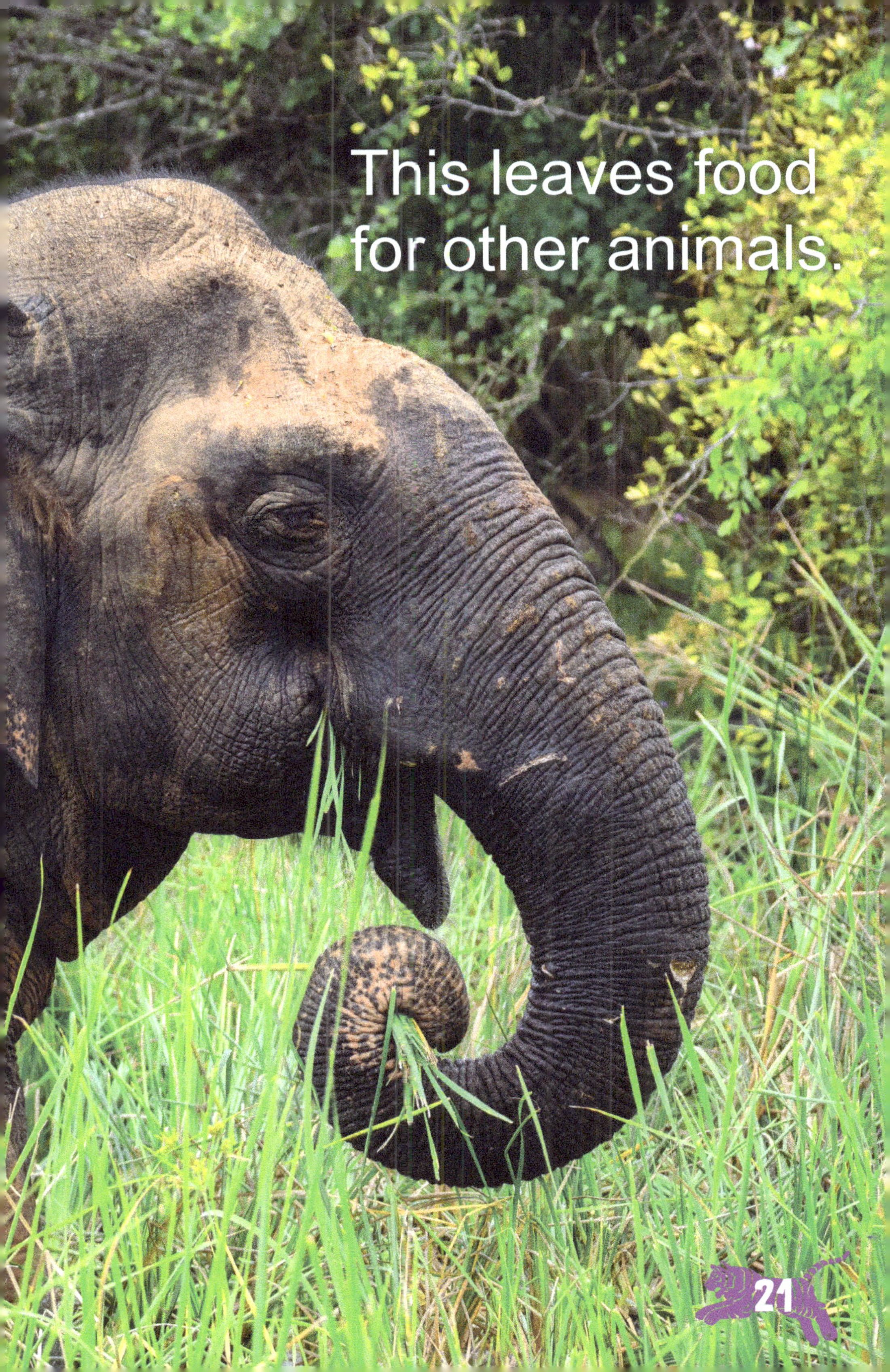

This leaves food for other animals.

Tigers have between one and seven babies.

Baby tigers are called cubs.

Cubs cannot see when they are born.

Male cubs grow faster than females.

Tigers become adults
at about four years old.

They live for
10 to 15 years.

Tigers may soon
be gone forever.

Too many people are hunting them.

Quiz

Test your knowledge of tigers by answering the following questions. The questions are based on what you have read in this book. The answers are listed on the bottom of the next page.

1 Are tigers the biggest cats in the world?

2 Do most tigers like to live alone?

3 Do some tigers live in forests?

4 Do tigers eat other animals?

5 Are baby tigers called cubs?

6 Can cubs see when they are born?

Explore other books in the
Animals That Make a Difference series

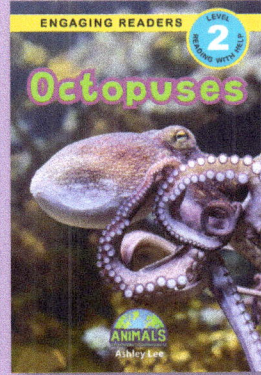

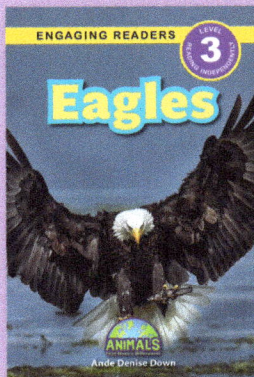

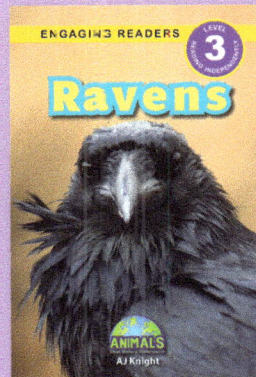

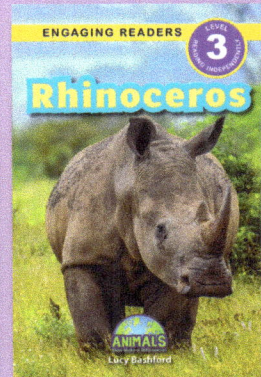

ENGAGING READERS · LEVEL 1 · READING TOGETHER — **Birds** — ANIMALS · Ashley Lee

ENGAGING READERS · LEVEL 1 · READING TOGETHER — **Ladybugs** — ANIMALS · Ashley Lee

ENGAGING READERS · LEVEL 1 · READING TOGETHER — **Squirrels** — ANIMALS · Ashley Lee

ENGAGING READERS · LEVEL 2 · READING WITH HELP — **Butterflies** — ANIMALS · Ashley Lee

ENGAGING READERS · LEVEL 2 · READING WITH HELP — **Frogs** — ANIMALS · Ashley Lee

ENGAGING READERS · LEVEL 2 · READING WITH HELP — **Octopuses** — ANIMALS · Ashley Lee

ENGAGING READERS · LEVEL 3 · READING INDEPENDENTLY — **Eagles** — ANIMALS · Ande Denise Down

ENGAGING READERS · LEVEL 3 · READING INDEPENDENTLY — **Ravens** — ANIMALS · AJ Knight

ENGAGING READERS · LEVEL 3 · READING INDEPENDENTLY — **Rhinoceros** — ANIMALS · Lucy Bashford

Visit www.engagebooks.com to explore more Engaging Readers.